Discovering Reptiles and Amphibians

Written by Stephen Caitlin

Illustrated by Pamela Johnson

Troll Associates

Library of Congress Cataloging-in-Publication Data

Caitlin, Stephen.
   Discovering reptiles and amphibians / by Stephen Caitlin;
illustrated by Pamela Johnson.
     p.   cm.
   Summary: Describes the characteristics of various reptiles and
amphibians such as the boa constrictor, monitor lizard, Gila
monster, and the tuatara.
   ISBN 0-8167-1753-2 (lib. bdg.)   ISBN 0-8167-1754-0 (pbk.)
   1. Reptiles—Juvenile literature.   2. Amphibians—Juvenile
literature. [1. Reptiles. 2. Amphibians.] I. Johnson, Pamela,
ill. II. Title.
QL644.2.C35 1990
597.6—dc20   89-4972

Imagine a time millions of years ago—a time when great, warm swamps covered much of the earth. The giant, land-roving dinosaurs did not exist yet. But the sea was filled with prehistoric creatures, swimming and searching for food.

One day, an amazing thing happened: a creature that looked a bit like a fish left the sea. It began to live on the swampy land.

This creature and the ones that followed it were the first amphibians. They were able to live in water and also on land. In fact, the name *amphibian* means "double life."

Many creatures we know today came from the first
amphibians. Birds, snakes, lizards, and mammals are a few such
animals. Scientists say these creatures evolved from amphibians,
which means they developed slowly over a very long time.

What is an amphibian? An amphibian has a backbone. It has moist skin without scales, and it has no claws. Most amphibians live part of their lives on land and part in the water.

Where can you find an amphibian? In many different places! Something stirs in the tall grass. Look closely—it is a small toad hopping along.

By the pond at night booms a loud croaking song. *Jug-o-rum!* sings a big bullfrog.

On a rainy day, a red salamander pokes its head from beneath a rock. The small creature decides it's a good day to hunt for worms to eat.

Deep within its burrow, or underground hole, lives another amphibian. It is called a caecilian (seh-SIL-yen). This strange animal looks like a big earthworm. The caecilian almost never leaves its burrow, so very little is known about this animal.

Scientists say there are three main groups of amphibians: frogs and toads, salamanders, and caecilians. Altogether there are about three thousand kinds of amphibians. They come in many different colors.

Most amphibians are rather small—about six inches (15 cm) long. The smallest is a tiny frog that could easily perch on your big toe. The biggest amphibian is a salamander that lives in Japan. This giant is five feet (1.5 m) long.

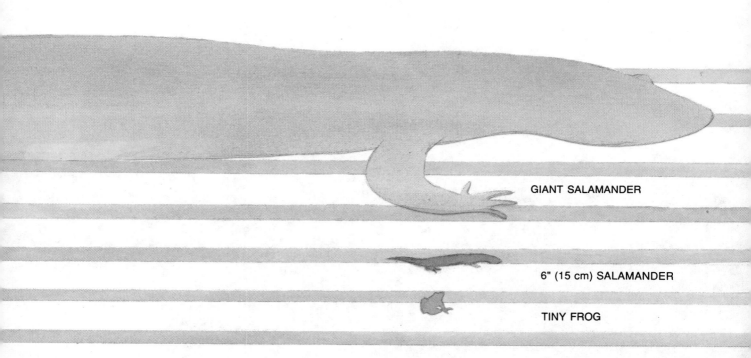

GIANT SALAMANDER

6" (15 cm) SALAMANDER

TINY FROG

Amphibians live almost everywhere, except in the frozen land of Antarctica. They especially like wet places to live, in or near streams, ponds, or lakes. This is because they must have a moist place to lay their eggs.

But certain amphibians are able to live on dry land. How do they survive? For weeks, they live underground in moist sand or dirt. When rain finally falls, out these amphibians come. Quickly, they lay eggs in any puddles they can find. The babies soon hatch and grow into adults—all before the puddles have dried up.

TOAD

All amphibians are cold-blooded. This means their body temperatures stay about the same as the air, water, or soil around them. In winter, when it is too cold for them, many frogs, toads, and salamanders hibernate. When they *hibernate,* their bodies go into a sleep-like state. Some salamanders and frogs dig deep into the mud at the bottom of a pond for their winter naps. Toads stay on land to hibernate.

When it is too hot or dry for them, some amphibians *estivate.* This word means the amphibians are not active—it is very much like hibernation.

FROG

Frogs and toads make up the biggest group of amphibians. Their strong hind legs help them to be good jumpers.

Can you tell the difference between a toad and a frog? It's not always easy, but there are a few ways to tell them apart. One difference is the kind of skin each has. A frog has moist, smooth skin. A toad's skin is usually drier and bumpier. Another difference is that the back legs of a frog are usually longer than a toad's. The frog's longer legs let it jump and swim better than a toad. Also, toads are usually fatter than frogs, and they can live in drier places than most frogs can.

As toads and frogs grow, their skins become too small for them. When this happens, these animals molt: their old skins split open. Within minutes, the frog or toad pulls off the too-small skin and eats it. The animal's new skin underneath fits just right.

Frogs and toads eat many insects. Hidden near a rock sits a brown and bumpy toad. It waits patiently for its dinner. When an insect flies near, out lashes the toad's long, sticky tongue. The toad almost never fails to catch its prey.

But the toad also has many enemies. Snakes, hawks, and skunks like to eat it. The toad's best protection is to hop away. It does have another way to protect itself, though. Its skin gives off a bad-tasting liquid, which most animals do not like to eat.

One of the most amazing things about amphibians is the change their bodies go through. This change is called *metamorphosis*. Metamorphosis takes place from the time amphibians are babies to the time they grow into adults.

The metamorphosis of a frog is fascinating to watch. Here is what happens. In spring, the grown-up male frog sings a deep, croaking song to attract a mate. The male has a large pouch on its throat that puffs up with air to make this loud sound.

The female lays great numbers of eggs in the water, which the male frog fertilizes. The eggs look like bunches of tiny grapes, and they have no shells. Instead the eggs are covered by a soft, jelly-like material. To grow into babies, the frog's eggs must be kept wet, just as all amphibians' eggs must.

A tiny tadpole, or polliwog, grows inside each egg. It has gills, like a fish, for breathing in the water. And each tadpole has a tail to help it swim.

The tadpole wriggles out of its egg. It is ready to begin its first stage of life in the water.

As the tadpole gets older, very important changes take place in its body. Skin grows over its gills. Lungs develop. The lungs will let the tadpole breathe air when it is ready to leave the water. Hind legs grow first, and then front legs appear. And all the while, the tadpole's tail is growing shorter until it's no longer there. The tadpole is not a tadpole anymore. It has changed into a frog and is ready for life on the land.

Salamanders also go through metamorphosis. Most salamanders lay their eggs in the water. The baby salamanders swim off through the water. Feathery-looking gills on the baby's head let the salamander breathe underwater. Legs and lungs soon grow to ready the salamander for life on the land.

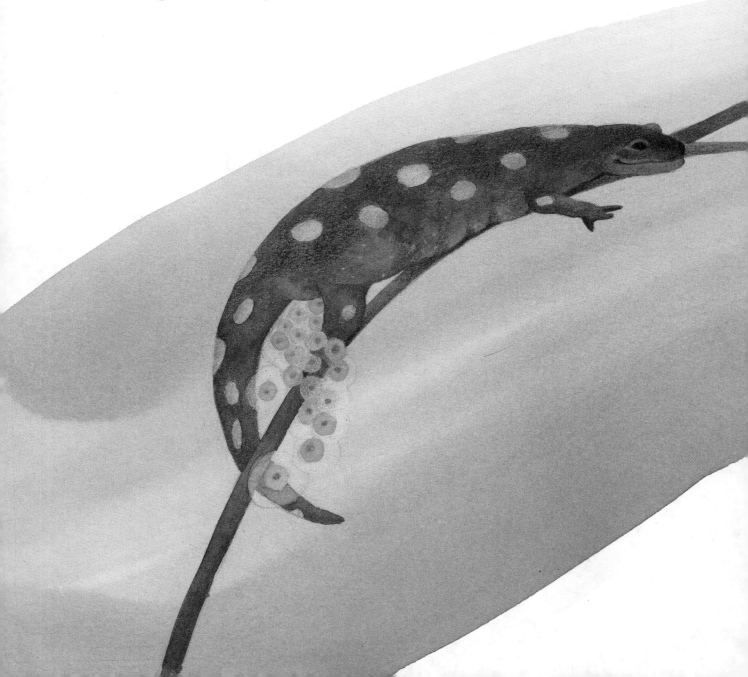

Some salamanders do not lose their gills. The adult mud puppy, a brownish-gray salamander, has three gills for breathing underwater, plus lungs for breathing air.

The most mysterious amphibian is the caecilian, living in its dark, underground tunnel. Scientists do know that caecilians lay their eggs in moist soil close to water. The mother curls her body around the eggs. When the babies hatch, they go to live in the water. As babies, their eyesight is good. But as they grow older, skin grows over their eyes, as if to get them ready for life in their dark burrows.

Scientists think there were once many more kinds of amphibians than there are today. Some died out, perhaps because the earth's weather had become drier.

A second very important reason that some amphibians did not survive has to do with a group of animals called reptiles. Reptiles developed from amphibians. Unlike amphibians, though, the reptiles did not need water in which to lay their eggs. Their tough, hard-shelled eggs would not dry out on land, and this made the reptile better able to live in dry places.

During the Age of Dinosaurs, giant reptiles called dinosaurs roamed the earth. These prehistoric creatures have long since disappeared, but some of their smaller relatives are alive today.

Altogether there are about six thousand kinds of reptiles. They make up four main groups. Lizards and snakes are the biggest group. The second group is called the crocodilians and includes alligators and crocodiles. Animals called caymans and gavials, which look a bit like crocodiles, are also part of this group. Turtles form the third group, and an animal called the tuatara (TOO-ah-TAR-ah) makes up the fourth group.

Reptiles are cold-blooded. And like amphibians, some reptiles hibernate in winter and estivate in dry, hot weather.

How do amphibians and reptiles differ? A reptile's dry, scaly skin is very different from an amphibian's moist, smooth skin. And a reptile does not go through metamorphosis—it is born with lungs to breathe air. The most important difference is between the eggs of these two kinds of creatures. An amphibian's eggs are soft and must be kept moist. A reptile's eggs have a tough shell and do not need to be kept wet.

Some reptiles make their homes in or near water. Crocodiles and alligators live in warm swamps and rivers. These animals have long, strong tails for swimming and fighting. Their powerful jaws and sharp teeth make them the enemies of fish, turtles, birds, raccoons, and other animals.

You can tell an alligator from a crocodile by the shape of their jaws. The crocodile's snout is thinner and pointier than that of the alligator, but no less fearsome.

The turtle is best known for the house it carries on its back. If danger is near, most turtles can pull their heads and legs into their safe, snug shells. The shell is made of plates, hard scales that have grown together.

The timid box turtle, with its pretty orange-and-black shell, roams the woods and meadows looking for insects and berries to eat.

In the ocean, a sea turtle swims slowly and gracefully along. She is heading for a sandy beach where she will lay her eggs.

BOX TURTLE

SEA TURTLE

Snakes are reptiles that have no legs. They live in many different places.

Some snakes lay eggs, and other snakes are born live from their mothers' bodies.

Baby cobras poke their way through their leathery eggs by using a special pointed tool called an egg tooth. The egg tooth grows on the tip of the baby's nose. When the babies hatch, they are already poisonous.

Most snakes are not poisonous, but they do like to eat other animals, including toads, mice, birds, and lizards.

INDIAN
PYTHON

Some snakes, such as the boa constrictor and the python, kill by squeezing or constricting their prey. The animal suffocates and is then eaten whole. The python, which can weigh up to two hundred fifty pounds (112.5 kg), can swallow a whole pig! The snake's lower jaw unhinges, letting its mouth open wide enough to eat such a big meal.

Lizards are reptiles that can be found in a great many places on earth. Most have four legs, although a few have no legs at all. Most also have movable eyelids, unlike snakes that cannot blink and seem to be staring all the time.

Many lizards have strangely interesting characteristics and habits. For example, the Australian fringed lizard has a long tail that it uses for balance. This creature can raise its front legs off the ground and run quickly along on its back legs. Some lizards, such as the chameleon, can darken or lighten their color in response to temperature or other environmental conditions. The American chameleon can change from bright green to brown.

AMERICAN CHAMELEON
(ANOLE)

KOMODO DRAGON
(MONITOR LIZARD)

Lizards can be fierce fighters and defend themselves in different ways. Monitor lizards have strong jaws for biting and long tails for striking their enemies. Other lizards can use their long, brittle tails to fool their enemies. If an enemy seizes it, the tail breaks off. The tail thrashes away with its attacker and the lizard crawls off to safety! Later, the lizard grows a new tail.

HORNED LIZARD

The horned lizard has one of the most unusual ways of defending itself. It can squirt blood from its eyes up to three feet away to scare off its enemies.

The Gila monster and the Mexican beaded lizard are the only poisonous lizards.

The tuatara is a reptile that looks like a lizard, but scientists think it is really more closely related to the dinosaurs. The sleepy tuatara likes to sun itself during the day. At night, it hunts for worms to eat.

Reptiles and amphibians are strange and yet beautiful creatures. Their many different habits and ways of life make them fascinating to study. And whether large or small, each of these animals plays an important part in the wonderful world of nature.